THE
LEGIONARY FORTRESS OF
CAERLEON-ISCA

Amgueddfa Genedlaethol Cymru
National Museum of Wales

THE
LEGIONARY FORTRESS OF
CAERLEON-ISCA

A Brief Account

By George C. Boon

The Roman Legionary Museum, Caerleon, 1987

First published in 1987
© National Museum of Wales

Production: Hywel G. Rees
Design: Penknife, Cardiff
Typesetting: Afal, Cardiff
Type: Baskerville 10/12 pt.
Paper: Huntergloss 170gsm
Printing: South Western Printers, Caerphilly

ISBN: 0 7200 0315 6

PART ONE

The Legionary Presence

Caerleon, from Christchurch.

Caerleon and its Garrison

The Welsh name records Caerleon's legionary past; but to the Romans it was *Isca*, after the river near by. The fortress was founded in A.D.74 or 75 and was maintained until about 290. All that we know of it comes from archaeological research, and although most sites have been built over there is more to see than at Chester or York, the other two permanent legionary fortresses in Britain.

Legio II Augusta, founded by Augustus out of the ruins of another Second Legion which had fought for him during the Civil Wars at the end of the Roman Republic, was one of thirty to which the security of the frontiers of the Empire was entrusted. At full strength, a legion numbered well over 5,000 effectives in a self-contained force, all Roman citizens and all infantry except for a small body of mounted scouts. In 43, the invasion-force had comprised four legions — of which this was one — and numerous auxiliary regiments of infantry (some part-mounted) and cavalry, nominally 500 strong and composed of non-citizen provincials. The First Thracian Regiment of Horse (*Ala I Thracum*) is in evidence at Caerleon and may have been cantoned with the legion in early days. Finds suggest that there may also have been a later auxiliary garrison. The legate or commander of a legion was a grandee, a senator with experience of a succession of civil and military posts. After three years or so, he might expect a provincial governorship or two and even a consulship. The most famous legate of *II Augusta* was the Emperor Vespasian (69-79), consul in 51, who had commanded it with distinction

5

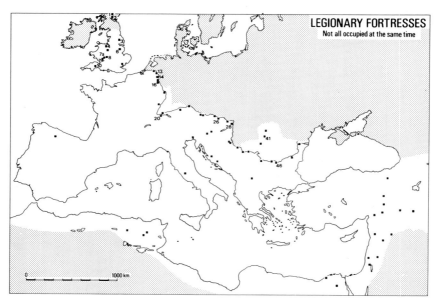

The numbers follow H. von Petrikovits, Innenbauten, Bild 1: 1. Inchtuthil; 2. Carpow; 3. York; 4. Chester; 6. Lincoln; 7. Caerleon; 7A. Usk; 8. Gloucester; 10. Exeter; 13. Xanten; 14. Neuss; 16. Bonn; 20. Vindonissa; 26. Carnuntum; 28. Budapest; 41. Alba-Iulia; 46. Novae.

Vespasian, A.D. 69-79.

in 43, and had gone on to conquer much of the south-west.

Towards 55 Exeter was chosen as our legion's base; and there in part it seems to have remained until the final conquest of Wales was taken in hand by the governor Frontinus in 74-5. The fierce Silures of south-east Wales, a thorn in the Roman side for a generation — at one time they had sheltered the celebrated Caratacus — had long since lost the south coast and everything east of the Usk; there was a legionary base at Usk town (*Burrium*), and auxiliary forts dependent upon it have been identified at Castlefield near Kenchurch, Abergavenny, Cardiff and possibly elsewhere;* there was also a landing place covered by soldiers stationed within the ramparts of a former Silurian coastal fortress at Sudbrook, connected with a ferry over the Severn to a station at Sea Mills in the estuary of the Bristol Avon. Caerleon, however, was still a virgin site. Coins and pottery earlier than the 70's are scarce there, and do not occur except mixed with later materials. Caerleon, indeed, was a replacement for *Burrium*, which had been a bad choice — that of a force making its way coastwards and not upstream — being subject to flash-floods and well beyond the tidal limit.

Bronze cooking-pan handle with the stamp of the Ala I Thracum. *The other stamp,* Maturus F(ecit), *is that of the Gaulish manufacturer. Museum Site, 1984.*

The estuarine siting of the Caerleon and Chester fortresses at the roots of the Welsh peninsula, and of auxiliary forts along the south, north and even the west coast of Wales, indicates the importance of river- and sea-communication. And from all these stations, roads led inland, on which some three dozen auxiliary forts were placed to control native movement, at about a day's march apart. These garrisons were phased out wherever

* There is some doubt as to whether the 1 ha enclosure at Coed-y-Caerau, on the ridge 4 km east of Caerleon, with wide views, is Roman.

and whenever practicable: their number reflected the exigencies of the past, not of the future which called for police-work among the conquered peoples. The warring-down of the Silures over a generation, and the harrying of the Ordovices of the north-west — Tacitus records the threat of genocide in the first case, and its actuality in the second, nothing new to Rome — had their effect in depressing population and morale alike. By the middle of the second century, few forts were left: garrisons were always needed elsewhere, and always there were problems of supply. Grain had to be imported from southern British producers who before the conquest had sold their surplus to the Continent — probably to the garrisons of the Rhine — and soon grudged delivering it as tax to 'remote and pathless places'. Other corn, as weeds in a charred sample from Caerleon reveal, originated in the Mediterranean region.

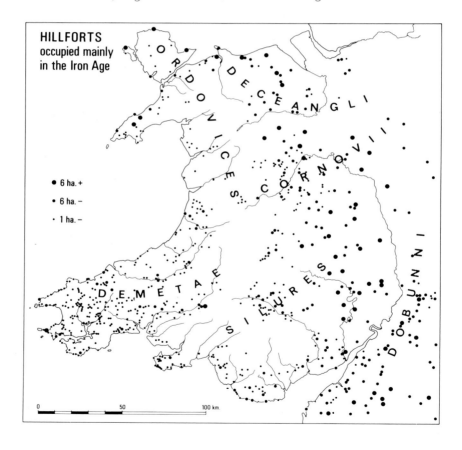

HILLFORTS occupied mainly in the Iron Age

● 6 ha. +
• 6 ha. −
· 1 ha. −

0   50   100 km.

The Site

A tongue of ground 15 m above sea-level projects south-eastward from
the 119 m Lodge Hill, crowned by the ramparts of another Silurian
stronghold given up, no doubt, when the Romans had reached the Usk
*c.*55. To the north-east runs the Afon Lwyd; to the south-west, the great
bend of the Usk was much sharper then. The site was grassy, scrubby:
chips, leaves, hazel-nuts, sedge, an ash-rake and ash, found with scraps of
torn leather tentage, betoken clearance ready for the surveyors by details
living in the eight-man ridge-tents known as 'butterflies' (*papiliones*). A
good supply of well-water existed; but a piped supply was obtained,
probably 10 km west of the fortress, where abundant springs at the rim of
the Coalfield were to be captured for Newport in modern times. A
massive circular structure employing legionary stamped bricks,

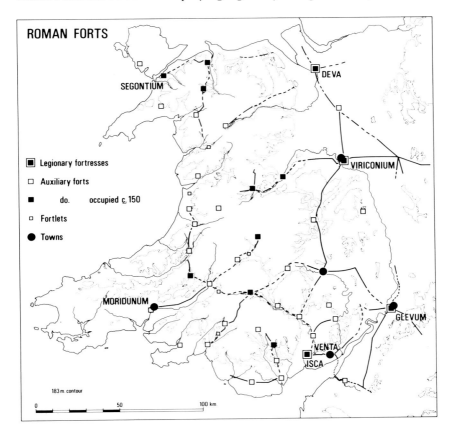

ROMAN FORTS

■ Legionary fortresses

□ Auxiliary forts

■   do.   occupied c. 150

▫ Fortlets

● Towns

SEGONTIUM

DEVA

VIRICONIUM

MORIDUNUM

GLEVUM

VENTA

ISCA

183 m. contour

0   50   100 km

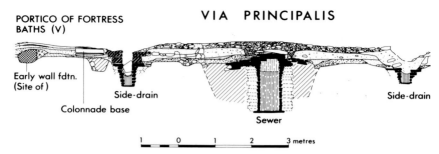

PORTICO OF FORTRESS
BATHS (V)

VIA PRINCIPALIS

Early wall fdtn.
(Site of)

Side-drain

Colonnade base

Sewer

Side-drain

discovered when Risca church was rebuilt in 1852, sounds like a catchment-tank for the powerful spring traversing that ground, like those of the Roman aqueducts of Cologne. An underground conduit, or pipeline like that of Chester fortress, would have led down a valley behind Lodge Hill to the Afon Lwyd and so round to the fortress; but nothing, in this altered terrain, has been seen.

A Bird's Eye View

Orderliness is the first and most abiding impression imparted by the plan, and was imposed by the need to house 64 centuries of men and their officers, and to provide for administrative and other buildings within a reasonable compass. The layout by cross-staff (*groma*) gave two main

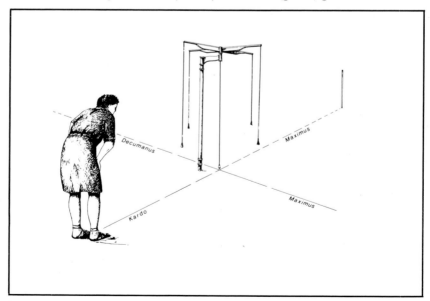

Groma *or cross-staff setting out the two main axes of the plan at right-angles.*

10

lines at right-angles, the initial station of the instrument in the middle of the cleared ground establishing the position of the entrance to the headquarters, which was to face south-east. The enclosure with its rounded corners ('hips' — *coxae*, designed to allow defenders to man these otherwise vulnerable points) measures some 495 by 420 m across the ramparts, making *Isca* a fortress of middling size — 20.5 ha, within extremes of 16.5 and 27 ha (Exeter and Bonn). On active service, a legion and some auxiliaries might crowd into an 8 ha camp; but in a permanent fortress room was needed for other accommodation there unnecessary. The baths (V)* take up a twentieth of the area, for example.

The layout is simple, governed by the *via principalis* running from the south-west to the north-east gate and by the other main streets. The headquarters (XV) in the middle and the tightly-set narrow rows of barracks at either end are noticeable. In more detail, we see (1) that the *via principalis* delimits a front division which is three lateral blocks (*scamna*) deep, and is bisected by the *via praetoria* running from the south-east gate up to the headquarters; (2) that the legate's residence (XX) is directly behind the headquarters, and so determines a central zone which is two blocks deep (as at Bonn); and (3) that the rear division, separated from the central zone by the *via quintana*, is also like Bonn in being only one *scamnum* deep; it is bisected by the *via decumana* running to the north-west gate.

The rear division is devoted wholly to barracks, twelve and twelve in facing pairs on either side of the dividing street, in all providing accommodation for four of the ten cohorts. Four more were similarly housed in the lowest *scamnum* of the front division. The other two cohorts lay to either side of the headquarters in XIV and XVII. In the former we note the large houses of the centurions and the wide spacing of the men's quarters, for this was the standard position of the first and most important cohort: we do not know which of the other nine occupied any given set of barracks. The spaciousness in XIV contrasts with the accommodation elsewhere, and arises from the temporary doubling of the size of legionary first cohorts about the time when *Isca* was established: Inchtuthil near Perth, occupied *c.*84-7 only, displays the ten barrack-blocks which the increased manpower demanded; but Gloucester, building for the Twentieth Legion in the 60's, cannot have had the space, and second-century fortresses such as Neuss on the Rhine do not.

Areas VII-XIII along the south-east side of the *via principalis* form a standard range of tribunes' or staff-officers' houses, for the senatorial

*These numbers are for ease of reference and have no ancient warrant.

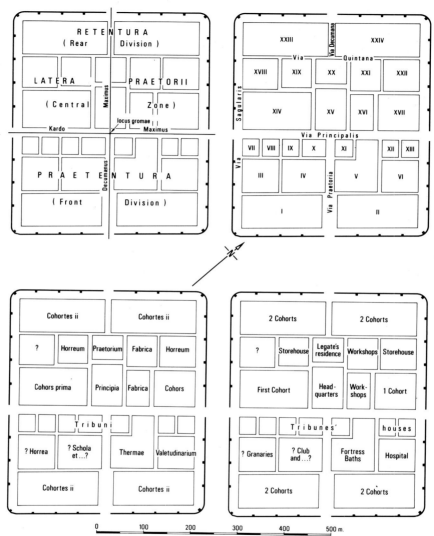

Key-plans of the fortress showing layout.

second-in-command; the camp-prefect or (later) legionary prefect, a professional risen from the ranks who was third-in-command but usually entrusted with the command when the legate was absent; and the five tribunes of equestrian rank who were really only aides-de-camp. From this row, the centurions' houses of the first cohort opposite, and the headquarters itself, we can easily see how the *via principalis* came to be

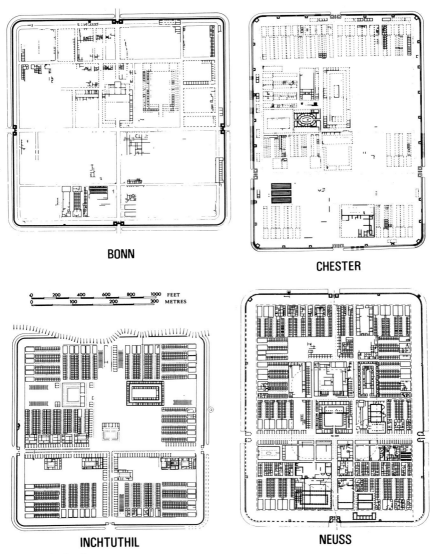

BONN

CHESTER

| 0 | 200 | 400 | 600 | 800 | 1000 | FEET |
| 0 | 100 | 200 | 300 | METRES |

INCHTUTHIL

NEUSS

Plans of other fortresses.

named. However, little is known of the 'tribunes' row'; and the range is unusually broken by the exercise-hall of the Fortress Baths (V), so called to distinguish them from extramural bath-houses. The hospital (VI) completes mention of buildings in the sinistral half of the front division;

13

in the dextral half, the two large areas III and IV retain their secrets, but III is near the south-west gate, and may have contained a row of three or four massive granaries, as at Chester in the corresponding space: the granaries preserved at Corbridge-on-Tyne give one an idea of what they would have been like, with ventilated raised stone floors and buttressed walls. Area IV, opposite the exercise-yard of the baths, may have held a club-house for other ranks; that is the suggested identification of a building at Inchtuthil in a similar position.

The headquarters (XV), legate's residence (XX) and barracks (XIV, XVII) in the central zone have already been mentioned, leaving five areas unexplained. Now a self-contained force needed extensive manufacturing and storage facilities, and it is not surprising to find that two or three of these areas seem to have been devoted to workshops of one sort or another (XVI, XIX, and XXI). As at Chester, Area XVIII may have contained another granary, though there are other possibilities; and XXII, a great storehouse planned round a courtyard perhaps used as a wagon-park, as in various other fortresses and in the same relative position at Budapest. The principal buildings are described below, in Part III (p.47).

The built-up area was insulated from the defensive zone by the *via sagularis*, named after the military cloak (*sagum*) which completed the uniform of soldiers assembling for duty there. The belt of ground beyond was devoted to storehouses set against or into the rampart, presumably for the heavy gear of the adjacent centuries; cook-ovens arranged in pairs like the barracks; cook-houses later built against the ground-floor chambers of the turrets; and, in each corner, a large latrine.

The defences consisted of a wide ditch, interrupted by causeways at the four gateways, and a rampart which was later faced with the stone wall still visible opposite the Amphitheatre and round past the south corner. There were corner- and interval-turrets, but we know very little of the gates. Such, in outline and without chronological differentiation, is the plan of *Isca* fortress.

The Surroundings

Caerleon was a nodal point of the road-system, and a key element was the bridge over the Usk. Of it we know nothing; but the tidal rise and race demanded massive masonry abutments and numerous piers with cutwaters up- and downstream, supporting a timber viaduct such as we see in the case of the Danube bridge on Trajan's Column; the suggestion is otherwise based on the remains of Roman bridges across the North Tyne near Chesters fort, and the Tyne itself at Corbridge.

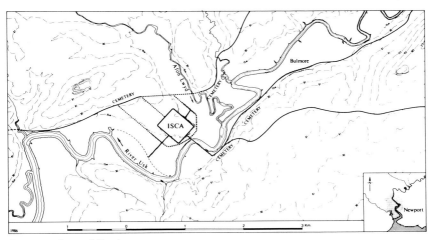

Roman environs of Caerleon.

Turning to the surroundings of the fortress as they eventually developed, we note firstly the bypass roads on the north-east and south-west, whereby traffic was excluded from the enclosure unless that were its destination. Indeed only the south-west gate (*porta principalis dextra*) seems to have been in much use: the south-east gate (*porta praetoria*) saw little but ceremonial comings and goings, if the thinness of the metalling outside is any guide; the north-east gate (*porta principalis sinistra*) seems to have been reduced to postern width at some date; and the scanty metalling of the *via decumana* suggests that the north-west gate (*porta decumana*), too, was little used.

Recent work shows that there was a considerable civil settlement (*canabae*) on the north-east beside the bypass road, bordering the marshes

Danube bridge, from Trajan's Column.

15

through which the Afon Lwyd made its way to a confluence with the Usk; the bath-house between the east corner and the south-east gate — the 'Castle' baths, so-called because they lie within the curtilage of the medieval castle — probably belonged to it. On the south-west, the bypass road ran beside a walled parade-ground north-west of the street leading down to the riverside wharves; to the south-east lay the Amphitheatre and various other buildings, notably a food-hall on the site of an early bath-house. Of domestic buildings there is little sign: a close group of six houses or shops lying at an angle to the bypass road, a square house doubtfully identified as the Caerleon *mansio* of the imperial posting-service (though lacking the private baths generally provided), and a few others quite widely spaced close the list. Three temples are attested by inscriptions but remain unlocated, though doubtless belonging to a suburb which may have been extensive south of the Amphitheatre. On the southern approaches to the Usk bridge traces of further buildings have been recorded, and there is a distinct roadside settlement at Bulmore 2 km to the east, also on the left bank of the Usk. On the whole, civil development in the vicinity of the fortress remained modest. At York or its predecessor Lincoln, the civil settlement grew into a thriving town which merited the title of colony; and at Alba-Iulia in Romania, for example, there was a native township in addition to the *colonia*, granted the rank of *municipium* in due course — the status, in Britain, of *Verulamium* (St. Albans). Manifestly, at Caerleon and Bulmore there were the beginnings of just such a development; but the commitments of the legion in northern Britain and elsewhere sufficed to stunt it. Also, the Silurian capital at Caerwent (*Venta Silurum*) was only 13 km to the east; and overseas trade on the western side of Britain, feeble by comparison with the south and east, was perhaps enough to support only one township. Evidence for foreign traders (from the Rhineland) in residence is derived from Caerwent, not Caerleon.

The fortress had two important cemeteries — the first on the lower slopes of Lodge Hill and extending beyond the Afon Lwyd to the east; the second on the valley-side between the Usk bridge and Bulmore, the inhabitants of which pillaged the monuments for the sake of their stone. Thus what until very recent years was regarded as a burial-club's mausoleum at Bulmore, excavated about 1815, turns out to have been merely a domestic building paved with re-used gravestones. The eight recovered formed a foundation-gift to the Legionary Museum in 1850.

Further Afield

The brickworks of the Twentieth Legion are at Holt, 12 km from Chester on the alluvium of the Dee valley, and take the form of a substantial bank of kilns and other plant. At Caerleon the equivalent may not have been so distant, for the local alluvium served for pantiles in the 18th century, and

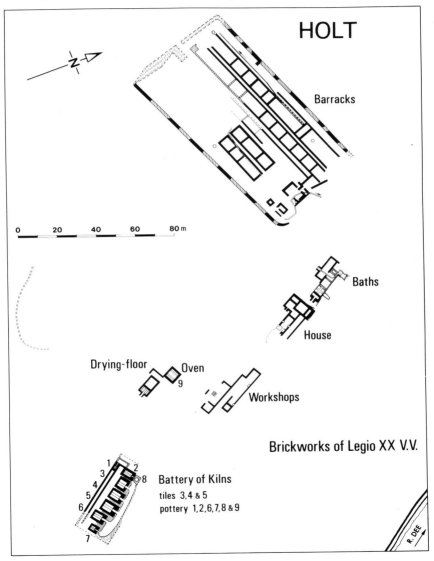

HOLT

Barracks

0   20   40   60   80 m

Baths

House

Drying-floor   Oven
9

Workshops

Brickworks of Legio XX V.V.

1
3   2
4   8   Battery of Kilns
5   tiles 3,4 & 5
6   pottery 1,2,6,7,8 & 9
7

R. DEE

17

the local clay for bricks as late as the 1950's. Lime-kilns, another massive installation, are best known from those of *Legio I Minervia* at Iversheim, on the limestone 30 km from the Bonn fortress. In our case, analysis shows that Lias limestone, argillaceous and making the strongest lime, was employed at the Fortress Baths as early as *c.*75, and furthermore that it was burnt with coal, the first-known industrial application of the mineral, which would have been dug from outcrops on the south or south-eastern rim of the South Wales Coalfield. The most likely source of Lias Limestone is perhaps the outlier at Lliswerry, east of Newport, where Roman objects have been found in quarrying, mainly to provide lime.

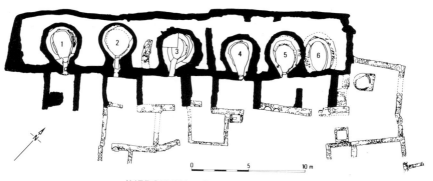

IVERSHEIM : **Battery of Lime-kilns**

Otherwise the quarries and the source of lead for piping and tanks can here receive but general mention. From the south side of the Severn came Bath Stone, and the figured grey-green Purbeck Marble from the Dorset coast was doubtless brought round by sea. Substitutes for Bath stone and the Mendip lead, which the legion had worked as early as 49 (though soon yielding its interests to government concessionnaires who could extract its silver), were eagerly followed up in South Wales. Sudbrook stone mixed with Bath Stone at the Amphitheatre, and lead from Draethen (with which a settlement at Lower Machen a few km west of Caerleon was connected), are cases in point.

The word *materia* ('building-timber') appears twice on part of a tiny wooden memorandum-tablet of soldiers' duties, stylishly inscribed in ink, from an early well on the Museum site. It serves to remind us that by far the most important building-material was wood, of which prodigious quantities were needed. Each of the 64 original barracks demanded a 500 m run of main timbers alone, and 150 ha of ancient wildwood must have

18

Purbeck marble bason, in the form of a shield with the Gorgon's head at the centre. 'Castle' Baths, 1849 (now exhibited at the Fortress Baths).

Lead water-main, 17 cm gauge. School Field, 1928.

*Memorandum-tablet (present length 8.5 cm)
referring to parties of men going to collect pay,
and being concerned with the building timber
(*materia*). Museum Site, 1985.*

been felled for the fortress as a whole, unless — as has been suggested —
timbers were salvaged from Usk and floated downstream for re-use.

This survey brings us now to the pastures (*prata*) for the mounts, the
draught-animals and the dairy and store cattle. That the area in question
lay on the Gwent Levels bordering the Severn can hardly be doubted.
They have long been praised for their excellent grazing, and reclamation
certainly began in Roman times and at legionary hands. At Goldcliff, 8
km south of the fortress, a 2nd-3rd century inscribed slab of Lias
Limestone (with the text all at one end so that the stone could be fixed in
the ground like a tombstone) was found well in advance of the present
sea-bank, and records the construction of a length of earthwork — ditch
or bank — by a century of the first cohort. The word *prata* does not
appear; but the inference is clear, and recent aerial survey in the vicinity
suggests that below the present irregular pattern of fields thereabouts a
more regular, rectangular system exists, indeed may still be glimpsed on
the eroding foreshore. That the stone should have come to light at
Goldcliff, a low knoll but one prominent in that flat terrain, is suggestive.
There if anywhere a boundary between legionary lands and those
allotted to the Silurian local authority might have been anchored; so that
the earthwork served a double purpose. Further large areas of Roman

reclamation have recently been recognised elsewhere along the coast as far west as the fringes of Cardiff, where the present regular drainage-pattern seems to continue the Roman. A legionary hand is surely detectable in the scale, regularity and perhaps the duration of the work, which seems mostly to have been done about the same period as that to which the Goldcliff stone belongs. There are several historical references to emperors calling on military labour to carry out such schemes either for the state's own benefit, or for that of favoured communities. Here, use or frequentation continued into the fourth century, after *Isca* had been abandoned.

Lastly, the Roman army, like its modern counterparts, provided for field-training and manoeuvres. On Llandrindod Common 90 km from *Isca*, eighteen small square earthworks, built for practice in technique, are recorded. They are not the only group of such camps in Wales, but are by far the biggest; the neighbouring fort of Castell Collen displays proof of legionary workmanship, and its baths are larger, and have a far larger latrine in particular, than an ordinary auxiliary regiment might be expected to possess. A route-march from Caerleon to this mid-Wales area would itself have counted as training, and would have shown the flag to native communities whose supervisory local garrisons had long since departed. Much nearer home, the old hillfort overlooking Caerleon on Lodge Hill would have been suitable for siege-practice, like Burnswark in Dumfriesshire.

A Legal Note

Conquered land became state property (*ager publicus*) under the control of the imperial treasury (*fiscus*); the surrendered inhabitants (*dediticii*) were bereft of all rights. Obviously the legion could and did seize and exploit all resources necessary for its maintenance, human as well as material; but it was not a corporate body in law, and could neither own, nor lease, nor apportion leases of land itself. When local communities (*civitates peregrinae*) were established on tribal lines within the conquered area, they were accorded tenure and enjoyment with rights (according to the jurist, Gaius) just short of outright ownership within carefully defined territories. The Roman state reserved the most valuable mineral rights, and on behalf of the legion would in our case have excepted also the various installations and lands described above, including the catchment-area of the water-supply and possibly the training-grounds. If any of these properties was given up, an inscription from Dalmatia reminds us that the land would have reverted to the procurator (or agent of the *fiscus*) for disposal.

Inscription found at Goldcliff in 1878, commemorating the construction of a drain or sea-bank: 'the Century of Statorius Maximus, of the First Cohort, 33½ paces.'

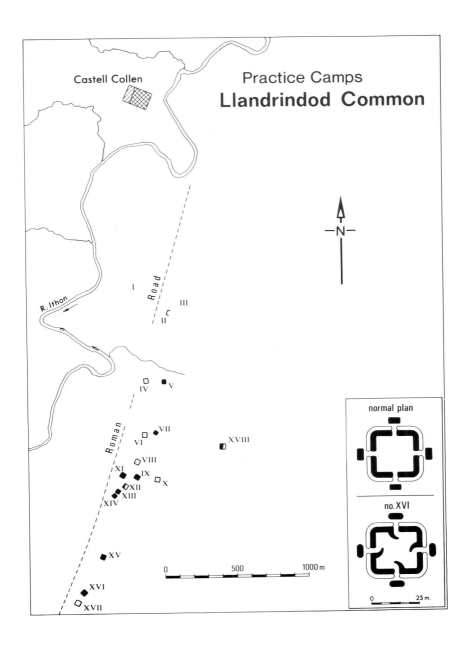

Castell Collen

Practice Camps
Llandrindod Common

R. Ithon

Road

I

III

II

Roman

IV
V

VII
VI

XVIII

VIII
XI
IX
X
XII
XIII
XIV

XV

XVI
XVII

normal plan

no. XVI

0   500   1000 m

0   25 m.

A lost inscription seen built into a stile near the Amphitheatre in 1798-9 bore the word *termin(us)* — 'boundary'. No piece of stone was worth carrying far at Caerleon; the boundary, accordingly, was near by. The stone presumably marked the limits of the legionary *territorium* outside the fortress, just a belt of land containing the parade-ground, the Amphitheatre, and perhaps other buildings: the one instance of the use of the word *territorium* in a legionary context, as likewise in an auxiliary one, implies that no greater extent of land was involved. The *canabae* or trading settlement would have been self-administering, nominally at least, and this implies a separate arrangement with the *fiscus*. As for the settlement at Bulmore, it is best understood as a *vicus* or village of the Silurian *civitas*, and not as legionary at all: the parallel with native townships near other fortresses is quite clear. To sum up, legionary holdings are best thought of as islets in a sea of native *territoria*, and not as wide territories centring on the fortresses. Indeed, the legion had no machinery for the administration of such large areas, and the word *territorium* does not appear in such a context. The Caerleon stone joins the few others, therefore, which throw light on the legal position of fortresses and their suburbs.

PART TWO

The Evolution of the Fortress

Archaeology and History

Our knowledge of the 'history' of the fortress concerns its structural evolution, the various phases of which can be put in order and approximately dated by archaeological means, even though the dates furnished by coins or other objects 'sealed' in or under a structure may turn out to be unreliably early. To extrapolate such datings into the field of military history is and always must be perilous. The only control we have, since there is little written history that is relevant, is the testimony of inscriptions.

We know less of the 'history' of *Isca* than the foregoing account may have implied. The reasons are twofold. Firstly, as a reservoir of trained manpower, the fortress saw many comings and goings, sometimes no doubt very prolonged; but they need not be strongly marked in the archaeological record of structures. Secondly, excavations have been going on at Caerleon for over 80 years, and their results are bound to reflect the varied ability of the excavators, and the advance of technique. In recent years, 'area' excavation has become possible, whereby the overburden is completely removed layer by layer, so that each period of construction or occupation can at last be studied in full, instead of merely glimpsed at depth in narrow trenches. The results have been predictably complex, and have encouraged a start on a fundamental reconsideration of the evolution of *Isca*. This cannot be completed for some time. Each generation builds its own fortress, and each builds differently.

The Early Fortress, c.A.D.75-122

The departure of substantial numbers of soldiers to assist in the building of Hadrian's Wall marks out a convenient first period of study. Of the earliest dispositions we know lamentably little, and nothing as to any accommodation for the auxiliary *Ala I Thracum*. We might guess, however, that an active campaigning base, such as *Isca* was at first, would have contained more granaries than a regular fortress: at Inchtuthil there were six, and room for eight; at Usk, besides the regular three, there were at least ten small or five large.

It has only lately been realised that over large areas of ground the earliest buildings may have eluded detection. Such is the conclusion drawn from the tribune's house on the Museum site (X), from three

Traces of the earliest, timber-built tribune's house on the Museum Site, 1985. Pits for the upright posts of a verandah, and a main wall-trench can be seen, with partitions on the right.

Hoard of gold coins, the latest of A.D. 74. Myrtle Cottage Orchard, 1939.

barracks in XVII, and from Barrack 9 of the Prysg Field series (XXIII), first sketchily traced in 1929. The new evidence calls for a reappraisal of findings in II, VI, XIV and XXIV, where the earliest structures may have escaped notice below the clean clay fallen from their walls, and soil brought in to raise the floor-level: what had been there identified as primary took the form of cobble foundations for a framed superstructure, which in X, XVII and XXIII is now known to have come in no earlier than about 85-100. In II, for example, an undetected early timber building might best account for a hoard of five gold pieces (together worth 125 *denarii*) found beneath the level of the stone-based Barrack 1. These coins end with a mint-fresh example of 74, and on overall value may be compared with the gross annual pay of a legionary at that date, 225 *denarii*, but subject to heavy deductions and compulsory savings. Perhaps the owner was a casualty in Frontinus' Silurian War.

Many of the barracks, officers' houses and other buildings were replaced, not necessarily on the same lines as before, *c*.100-120. The cobble foundations had proved inadequate, and a few courses of masonry were substituted to carry the entire timber frame clear of the ground; the mid second-century dates which were thrown up by a study (published in 1972) of the original excavation-records and the finds evidently concern further changes. Some of the differences in spacing may have arisen

SECTION ACROSS S.W. DEFENCES

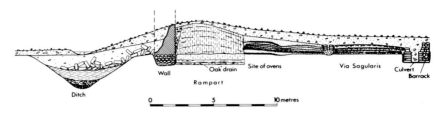

because various centuries were absent: a strong detachment or vexillation served in the Emperor Domitian's German campaign which culminated in 83, for example. Fresh work is urgently needed in XIV, and might be directed to ascertaining the original arrangement of the first cohort's accommodation, and the likely date of its reduction once more to normal size (480 effectives).

Neither the hospital or the main workshops (XXI) progressed beyond the timber-framed, stone-silled design; but some buildings were constructed — or at least planned — in masonry throughout. The great hall of the headquarters may never have been completed to the intended elevation, though other parts of the great building certainly were. The legate's residence was not the first building on its site, and may well overlie primary timber remains; but another stone building, the large hall

Foundations for a timber superstructure, Barrack I. Prysg Field, 1927.

Luna marble inscription, 120 by 145 cm. The Legion dedicates the south-west gate (?) to the Emperor Trajan, A.D.100. Notice the later cutting of the last stroke of the numeral. School Field, as found, 1928.

in Area XIX, was primary. Certainly primary are the baths, where the elaborate structure of cold, warm and hot halls was complete and functioning by the year 80, and was soon extended by the addition of a swimming-pool on one side, and by laying out a covered exercise-hall on another. Such was the importance paid to the cleanliness of the crowded soldiery, to their comfort, and to their need for relaxation.

The original defences would have had a timber palisade with wide embrasures (such as we see on Trajan's Column), and timber turrets and gates probably of openwork construction above rampart-walk level. The wall with its attached turrets and gates was 1.5 m thick, and was added not long after 86, the date of a mint-fresh coin from the foundation-trench of the south corner-turret — evidence borne out from excavations there in 1909 and by later work in XVII and XXIII. On the Chester and York analogy, the handsome white Luna marble dedication to the Emperor

Trajan in his third consulship, A.D.100, found re-used as paving in XIX, its corner already gone, may have adorned the south-west gate only 120 m away. This slab seems to have been ordered with its text ready-cut, for the consular numeral has been changed from II to III. The seas were closed from mid-November to early March, and a stone completed late in the season would have had to wait until shipping resumed, indeed perhaps until the safe period for navigation was reached in late May, before being conveyed to Caerleon.

The Extramural Area

Nothing is known of early *canabae* on the north-east side, where the early rubbish-dumps may have accumulated, if waste material including the neck of an amphora from Rhodes, bearing the legion's title, is so to be explained. On the south-west, however, the area in front of the defences revealed traces of timber sheds resting on the ground, probably thatched, as much as 40 m long and 10 m wide: they seem to have belonged to a supply-base. The erection of baths marks the end of this phase south-east of the street down to the river, and the Amphitheatre was obviously squeezed in between it and the defences: the inference must be that the land north-west of the street was still occupied by the sheds. About 90, however, a disastrous fire swept through the extramural area and also consumed the wooden seating of the Amphitheatre; fancy suggests that it may have started through neglect of the malting-process going on in one of the timber buildings, where beer was to be brewed: it was this burnt grain which, upon study, revealed the weed-seeds of Mediterranean origin mentioned above.

The full complexity of the early timber buildings could not be recorded when the sports-field was laid out north-west of the road in 1962. However, it was found that the shallow impressions of the sleeper-beams of the earliest series (not quite parallel with the fortress) were demarcated from a very large building (60 by 20 m) near the defences by a small ditch, crammed with comminuted samian pottery which, perhaps, had been stored within. Later buildings had uprights set individually into square pits, and were aligned at the same angle as persisted in the case of a row of shops fronting obliquely on to the bypass road, as if that had truncated earlier buildings. The same alignment is exhibited by the early baths near the Amphitheatre. The reason for the divergence from the fortress-alignment is obscure, but points to there having been a different authority in charge of the extramural cadastre, as might well have been the case if the position of the *canabae* was regularised by reference to the procurator of the *fiscus*.

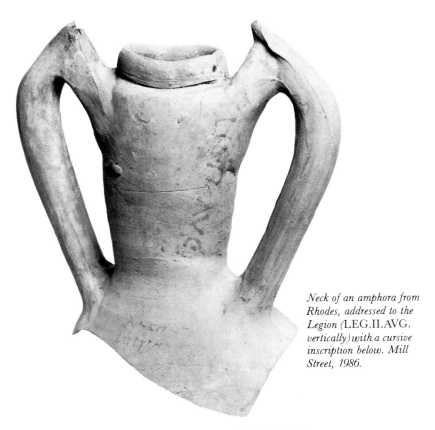

Neck of an amphora from Rhodes, addressed to the Legion (LEG.II.AVG. vertically) with a cursive inscription below. Mill Street, 1986.

The Second-Century Fortress, c.A.D.122-96

The Hadrian's Wall commitment was scarcely over before the legion was involved in the advance into Scotland and the construction of the Antonine Wall in the early 140's, and in garrison-duty here and there in the north. It seems that the fortress can have been only lightly garrisoned for long periods in the second century; but men sent north for building-work may have returned to base in the winter.

Absences may possibly be reflected in the buildings of the fortress by decay, or by a varying incidence of occupation as attested by the amount of domestic refuse accumulated in the barracks — pottery and food-bones, chiefly. Thus in XXIII it might be said that Barracks 6 and 7 contained a great deal, but others less, although the material is demonstrably contemporary. But the interpretation is far too simplistic, for two other factors — ancient and modern — enter in. Some centurions

31

may have been more insistent than others that the barracks be kept clean; and for that matter some blocks — e.g. Barrack 9 — were but sketchily excavated originally. A better indication is renewal of structures; and as we have already seen, there is quite wide evidence for it in barracks during the middle years of the century. The baths, the hospital and the workshops (XXI) were likewise affected, and there was work later on at the headquarters, where the chapel of the standards was restored apparently *c*.176-80. It is possible, nonetheless, to exaggerate the effects of the long-term northern commitment. There seems to be a considerable overall mass of finds from Caerleon to attest a strong occupation in the second half of the century. For that matter, the fort at Castell Collen was restored by a vexillation of the legion in that period; and if that fort was chosen as the headquarters of troops on manoeuvres as suggested above, the obvious implication is that there were troops, and there was time, to spare for such things. The garrison at Caerleon, however, need not have been wholly legionary.

Inscription from Castell Collen fort, Llandrindod Wells, recording restoration by a Vexillation of the Legion. Found 1956.

The Extramural Area

The reshaping of the south-western suburb does not seem to have been taken in hand until nearly fifty years had passed after the fire of *c.*90; and on this showing we do discern the impact of the northern commitment. The wall enclosing the parade-ground, the completion of the bypass road, the erection of the 'oblique' houses or shops beside it, together with the extensive repairs of the Amphitheatre and the demolition of the early baths near by, all seem to belong to the years towards 140; the erection of the food-hall on the baths site, and the construction of stone quays beside the river, were yet to come. As to the settlement on the north-east of the fortress, the first developments seem to be of a similar period to those outlined above. In particular, the bypass road was probably also laid out towards 140.

Septimius Severus, A.D.193-211.

The Third-Century Fortress, c.A.D.196-293

Civil war, which had brought Vespasian to power, now endued Septimius Severus with the purple. The assassinations of Commodus and Pertinax had led the Governor of Britain, Clodius Albinus, to make his bid for the throne, and he was briefly recognised by Severus as a colleague while another rival was eliminated. In 196, Albinus crossed to Gaul with most of the army of the province, but the hard-fought battle of Lyons ended his hopes in 197. That the Second Augustan suffered heavily must be certain; but brought up to strength or else brigaded with other forces it took part in preparations for Severus' renewed campaigns into Scotland, in the

IMPERATORES CAESARES·L·SEPTI	MIVS SEVERVS PIVS	PERTINAX AVG·ET	· M· AVRELIVS
ANTONINVS AVGETP·SEPTIMIVS	CETA NOBILISSIMVS	CAESAR	
VETVSTATE CORRVPTVM ٬			RESTITVERVNT ٬

Frieze, partly restored, recording the reconstruction of some part of the Headquarters, c.A.D.198-209. Churchyard, c.1850. Only the second panel is preserved, length 119cm.

advance itself, and in garrison-duties before and afterwards, indeed for some years after Severus died at York in 211.

The years after 197 are very interesting at Caerleon, where we have three inscriptions datable to 198-209; but it is unfortunate that we cannot date them more closely, because work at the Fortress Baths has brought to light a curious phase of demolition towards the year 200 — soon countermanded, but leaving its mark at the swimming-pool where the flagged lining was removed. The demolition of such an important building should tell us that the garrison was under orders to leave *Isca* for good; and it so happens that in *c.*208 work began on a new 13 ha fortress at Carpow at the mouth of the Tay, for a mixed garrison apparently of the Second Augustan and Sixth Legions, though occupation cannot have lasted beyond *c.*215. It is possible that *II Augusta* had been marked down for dispersal among various stations in the north, including Carpow.

Another explanation arises from the division of Britain into two provinces — *Britannia Superior*, or Upper Britain, with two legions at Caerleon and Chester; and *Britannia Inferior*, or Lower Britain, with one legion at York. The date of the division is disputed; if it occurred soon after the victory of Severus at Lyons as the historian Herodian says, the very senior rank of early governors commemorated in *Inferior* implies that the legionary garrison was at first divided differently, with two legions there, and only one legion in *Superior*. Demolition at Caerleon lends colour to that possibility.

We revert to the inscriptions. One is a very important slab from a long frieze commemorating the restoration of some ruinous part of the headquarters by Severus and his two sons, Caracalla and Geta; the other two are dedications by the legionary prefect and his two sons — the parallel could scarcely have been unintentional. Such a man must have been among the officers introduced into *II Augusta* after Lyons. The next inscription, about half preserved on a very weathered slab of Bath Stone, was found outside the fortress in 1603. It may have commemorated the rebuilding of the south-west gate, which had the projecting side-towers typical of defences of the late second or early third century rather than before; it belongs to the sole reign of Caracalla (212-17), and would have replaced the Trajanic marble inscription already mentioned. By this period, it is clear, the legion was largely at home: Tiberius Claudius

Altar to Salus Regina *by P. Sallienius Thalamus, Prefect of the Legion, and his two sons. Headquarters. Churchyard, 1845.*

Paulinus, who was Governor of Lower Britain in 220, would have held his command of *II Augusta* about 214-17; his statue was erected at Caerwent by the local authority, for whom he had evidently performed a signal service.

Repairs to the Fortress Baths were put in hand and refurbishment throughout the fortress is marked by roof-tiles — no bricks — bearing the legionary stamp LEG II AVG ANTO or the like, *viz.* with the addition of the title *Antoniniana*, 'Antoninus' Own', awarded by Caracalla to most regiments and borne in Britain from 213 to 222, when it was replaced by

35

Pedestal inscribed by the Silurian local authority at Caerwent in honour of Tiberius Claudius Paulinus, Legate of the Legion, subsequently a provincial governor in Gaul, and in Britain A.D. 220. Found 1903 (St Stephen's church, Caerwent).

another, *Severiana* in honour of Severus Alexander, emperor 222-235 (tile-stamps at Caerleon reading LEG II AV S or the like seem to represent it, but are rare). The occurrence of these datable tiles indicates which buildings were reroofed or patched: among the latter are the barracks of Area XXIII, unoccupied but kept in weatherproof condition against the return of the cohorts concerned (Barrack 12, however, was dismantled). In II there is plentiful evidence of reroofing, and XIV, XVII and XXIV were also fully maintained; a hint that occupied barracks may not have been so densely inhabited as before, however, is suggested by work in XVII, where one block was rebuilt as a series of single apartments rather than pairs of cubicles, a design akin to the chalet rows at late Roman *Segontium* (Caernarvon) and elsewhere.

Representative tile-stamps of the Legion (scale: ¹/₂).

In these circumstances, the closure of the baths not long after 230 — the last two coins attributable to loss during normal bathing activities being of Alexander — is strange. Perhaps the garrison was, after all, too reduced for the continued operation of the great hypocausts with their enormous consumption of brushwood and timber, which must have been brought from ever more distant sources unless coppicing was practised on an extensive scale. An extensive but undated reconstruction of the smaller 'Castle' baths may perhaps belong to this time.

Be this as it may, the continued residence at Caerleon of the administrative staff is betokened by inscriptions of 234 and 244, when the chief centurions of the time honoured the birthday of the Eagle (September 23—Augustus's); and next there is an important slab of 253-8,

Inscription, (71 × 94 cm), recording the rebuilding of barracks for the Seventh Cohort, c.A.D.253-8. Castle Mound, c.1845.

which records the total rebuilding of barracks for the seventh cohort, which had presumably returned to base after a long absence. Comings and goings about this time are illustrated by an inscription of 255 found at Mainz, telling of the vexillations of the Second and Twentieth Legions which are later traceable in the Balkans and probably never saw South Wales again. Nor indeed need we look so far afield, for the legion was clearly active in south-west Wales too.* Ballast of shattered Pembrokeshire slate — a material which had never been used at the fortress otherwise — was spread as metalling behind the quay-walls at last constructed on the riverbank south-west of the fortress in the later third century. Men may have been sent down to the south-west in connexion with a re-opening of the gold-mines at Dolaucothi near Llandovery, or with the defences of the little town of *Moridunum* (Carmarthen), where occupation persisted into the fourth century and where an honorific inscription of fourth-century date is known. The roads, too, were kept in order for the sake of patrols from as early as the time of Gordian III (238-44) as the inscribed milestones indicate; they include four of the Gallic separatist rulers Postumus (260-8) and

---

*An Antoninian tile attributed to the fort at Pennal on the north side of the Dyfi estuary is no longer regarded as an authentic find from there.

Third century Usk quay, with traces of a timber apron, south-west of the fortress, 1963.

Milestone of Victorinus, height 119 cm, A.D. 268-70, from Pyle, Port Talbot (Royal Institution of South Wales, Swansea). Found c. 1845.

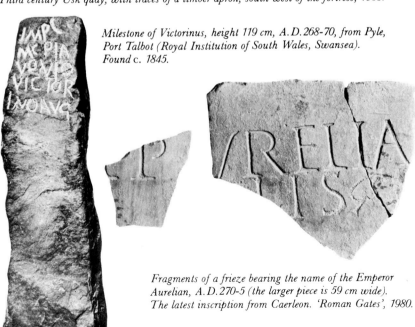

Fragments of a frieze bearing the name of the Emperor Aurelian, A.D. 270-5 (the larger piece is 59 cm wide). The latest inscription from Caerleon. 'Roman Gates', 1980.

Victorinus (268-70) and run eventually down to Constantine II, towards 340. The evidence of roadworks in North Wales is not dissimilar.

A single stamped tile seems to preserve the title, abbreviated to VI as if for *Victoriniana* ('Victorinus' Own', since the legion does not seem to have borne the title *Victrix*), and tells of roof-maintenance as late as 270, likely in view of the roadworks which would have been organised from *Isca*, where accommodation would have been repaired for the men involved. The latest imperial inscription — a recent find from XVII where a few fragments from a frieze occurred — names the Emperor Aurelian (270-75) and belongs to 274-5 after the recovery of Britain from Tetricus, last of the Gallic usurpers. Within fifteen years the fortress was to be abandoned.

Portico of Macellum, *near the Amphitheatre, 1955.*

The Extramural Area

Numerous Antoninian tiles structurally used at the Amphitheatre, especially in the niche at the back of the arena-level chamber on the east side, indicate a restoration *c.*213-22 or later; the food-hall adjacent may have been built, or was at least reroofed, about the same time. There is epigraphic evidence from the suburb too, in the form of a neat tablet commemorating the restoration of the temple of Diana by the legionary legate, perhaps by way of thanks for splendid hunting in the district, *c.*250: Postumius Varus, the man in question, rose to be Prefect of the City of Rome in 271. The building eludes discovery, as does the temple of the Syrian deity, Jupiter Dolichenus, popular in the third-century army (though this is the only legionary instance in Britain). Like the other inscription in honour of Diana, it probably came from the vicinity of the Amphitheatre. Somewhere, too, there was a *Mithraeum*, also likely to be of the third century. The inscribed pillar which names the Unconquered Mithras was found in the 'Castle' baths.

Otherwise the period was one of drastic change in the south-western suburb. Towards 240 the group of houses or shops set obliquely to the bypass road was demolished and the road itself was heavily remade: we may remember the testimony of the milestones from the time of Gordian III along the south coastal route and the Usk-Towy corridor. The

Tablet recording the restoration of the Temple of Diana by T. Flavius Postumius Varus, vir clarissimus, *c.A.D.250. Found S.W. of the fortress, 1603.*

Rebuilt drain beside the bypass road on the S. W. of the Parade Ground, with road-metalling to R., 1958.

courtyard house or supposed *mansio* of the post, with a stone-slabbed roof, was built squarely on to the new street. The riverside quays have already been mentioned; the last work at the riverside was the construction of a timber stage in front of the stonework, a vain attempt to overcome silting. Areas of hard-standings, but little else except a building — perhaps a boat-house since it was open to the river, and was traversed longitudinally by a box-drain — were discovered; all timber-framed buildings would have been swept entirely away.

When the bypass road was remade, the drain which flanked it was necessarily also raised, huge puddingstone blocks being employed for its new sides. This type of stone, local, had hitherto seen little use at the fortress; and since similar blocks were found in use as sills for timber buildings in an extension of the settlement on the north-east side of the fortress, a date towards 240 may well apply to that development also. The separate *vicus* at Bulmore is in the main of second and third-century date, and had its own little cemetery of inhumations, one in a Bath Stone coffin.

The End of the Legionary Isca

In the Amphitheatre Report, Sir Mortimer Wheeler opined nearly 60 years ago that 'the significant history of Roman Caerleon ends with the third century'. That remains true. Signs of a fourth-century presence outside the fortress are almost non-existent; inside they are scattered, concentrating here and there, as it may be in a patched-up barrack-block, to demonstrate habitation which (in default of recognisable military accoutrements) must be classed as civilian, indeed as native. In Area V the walled exercise-yard of the baths was turned into a stockyard where small cattle of about the same size as a Kerry cow were kept in a portico, partly rehabilitated as a byre. The coins from this area run down to the 370's, as they do in Area II where a centurion's flat was re-roofed with stone slabs. In Area XVII, two rooms in a barrack contained large cesspits. The latest coins from the fortress are two of the Theodosian dynasty, one of *c.*388-95, from Area XVI.

Not only does the continuous military history of *Isca* cease towards the end of the third century; it ceases in dismantlement. Several important buildings — the headquarters, the hospital, the legate's residence probably, and parts of the baths were levelled at a date indicated by coins of the British usurper Carausius, almost all struck before 290-1, occurring

beneath rubble. Of these one was found in the ashes of a fire lit at the entrance to the chapel of the standards in the headquarters, on a surface from which the flagstones had already been removed. No doubt there was much valuable material to scavenge throughout the fortress, but fragments of bronze statuary from the headquarters, near the chapel, are not to be explained as relics of imperial statues left standing when the garrison withdrew. Sacred and valuable as these effigies were, they would not have been left to the mercy of demolition-gangs. Thus at *Novae* fortress in Bulgaria, it seems to have been the practice over a long period to collect and store in the treasuries beside the chapel fragments of statues, probably of emperors who had suffered *damnatio memoriae*

Fragmentary pteryx*, length 27 cm, from the skirt of an Imperial statue in full armour. Headquarters, 1969.*

at the hands of their successors. The young Geta, murdered in 212 by his brother Caracalla, is among the number of these, his name being erased from every monument throughout the Empire, as two Caerleon stones demonstrate.

The late Roman strongholds in South Wales were walled Caerwent, occupied until the end of the fourth century, and the fort at Cardiff which had been newly erected towards 280, but was abandoned by 380 (for there are no Theodosian coins from it). A building on the shore at Cold Knap, Barry, was begun under the British usurper Carausius or his successor Allectus but was left incomplete. Its plan, with wings around a courtyard and more spacious accommodation facing the sea, suggests the residence of a high civil or military officer. It may be added that an original and wiser counsel has prevailed over the interpretation of an inscribed mosaic panel at the hilltop temple of Nodens at Lydney, further up the estuary, where the abbreviated word REL is now at last accepted as having to do with 'religion' rather than a naval repair-base (*reliquatio*).

Coin of Carausius (x2), commemorating the Legion (LEG) II AVG, *and showing its Capricorn emblem. London mint.*

The End of the Legion

A coin of Carausius honours *Legio II Augusta* among other legions (including vexillations) under his control, and is the latest evidence for its existence in its old form. By *c.*290 the strength of the body remaining at Caerleon must have been much reduced by the detachment of vexillations which never returned. It is thought in the light of the archaeological evidence mentioned above that the remaining force was sent to south-east Britain in order to counteract the invasion threatened by Maximian, Diocletian's colleague in the west, in 289. In 296, when Maximian's junior colleague, the Caesar Constantius I (father of

44

Constantine the Great) successfully did invade, our legion was probably involved.

The *Notitia Dignitatum*, a fifth-century almanac, lists in an obsolete section the command of the Count of the Saxon Shore, in which *Legio II Augusta* figures as one regiment among others. The editor of the printed text places it at the 2 ha fort of Richborough, but (at most) only a detachment can have been there; the rest may have been divided between various forts and towns of the south-east in a manner typical of the late empire, and for that matter elements may have been billeted at Caerwent and also at Cardiff. Other units traceable back to *Legio II Augusta* can be found in continental sections of the *Notitia*; some may have crossed to the Continent with the last British usurper, Constantine III, in 407.

It is noteworthy that coins of the House of Theodosius (including some of Honorius, entering Britain after the suppression of yet another continental usurper, Eugenius, in 394) are common at Caerwent and (presumably derived thence) appear very thinly scattered along the southern seabord as far west as Carmarthen, which has recently yielded an authentic specimen. In North Wales, however, coins of Honorius are lacking. Caerwent, it seems, was the western bastion of a final reorganisation of Roman defences in Britain by the Vandalic generalissimo of Honorius, Stilicho, in *c.*399. Possibly, therefore, a few remnants of the proud force founded by Augustus over 400 years before participated in this short-lived arrangement; but the fortress at Caerleon no longer had any part to play.

From Isca to Caerleon

By the end of the fourth century, Caerleon must have been an almost deserted ruin. Its parish church is dedicated to S. Cadoc, one of the great Celtic saints of the sixth century; there is no work visible anywhere near that date, but a tenth-century cross with a wheel-shaped head is known from Caerleon and points to the existence of a religious community linked in some way with Cadoc's monastery at Llancarfan in the Vale of Glamorgan. A stone-lined grave containing the skeleton of a woman datable to these so-called 'dark ages', found in Area XVII only 150 m from the church, may be connected with this shadowy settlement. We close with the famous visit in 1188 of Giraldus Cambrensis, companion of the Archbishop of Canterbury on the latter's tour through Wales preaching the Crusade. His impressions of Caerleon are full of learned echoes and with details taken from Geoffrey of Monmouth's imagined tale; but among the *immensa palatia* he mentions, the Fortress Baths were not indeed to be demolished for a century to come, when the materials were taken very largely for the castle of the Marcher Lordship — its original great mound was already there in Giraldus' day — and perhaps for the Cistercian abbey of Llantarnam ('Caerleon Abbey'), a daughter-house of Strata Florida.

RAMPART-BUILDINGS AND BARRACKS IN WEST CORNER

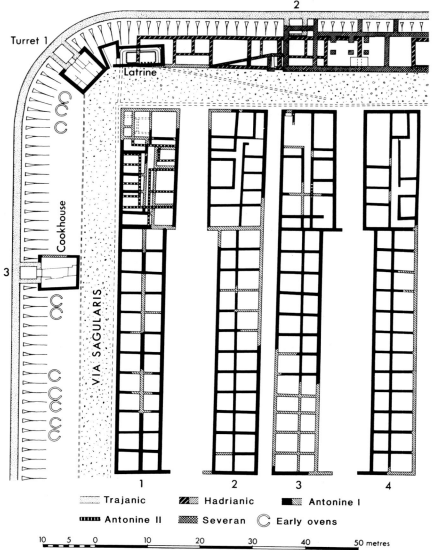

Trajanic Hadrianic Antonine I
Antonine II Severan Early ovens

PART THREE
Notes on Selected Buildings

Living Accommodation — Barracks (XXIII, etc)

At the time of writing, Caerleon still possesses, in the west corner of the fortress, the only foundations of a legionary barrack-block of imperial age to be seen in Europe. The other three blocks laid out over the ancient foundations at the modern ground-level in Area XXIII — the Prysg Field site of 1927-9 — are 'ground-plans in stone' and combine with the deeper foundations nearest the south-west side of the defences to show an arrangement in facing pairs, providing a narrow court or neighbourhood where the great society of the legion was broken down into groups of messmates who could mix and feel at home together. In essence the arrangement — of three such pairs for every ordinary cohort — stems from the tactical unit of two centuries or maniple, of which we read in Republican history; but even by Caesar's time the cohort had long supplanted it as a field formation and it is no longer mentioned in a strict sense thereafter. The two centuries commanded by the chief centurion are another waif of the manipular system, as is the pairing of the ward-cubicles in the hospital (p.54) and, for that matter, of the centurial bread-ovens behind the rampart.

The barrack-block (*centuria* — the same word as applied to the century of men: it occurs in the inscription recording the rebuilding of barracks for the seventh cohort, p.38) is almost 74 m long, and of this a third forms the centurion's flat, which runs to the full width of 11.5 m or so; the men's quarters are narrower by the width of a verandah. The walling exposed is really below floor-level, so that no doorways are apparent; but the overall design is clear enough, despite alterations in the centurion's section. There the original plan allowed for as many as a dozen rooms of varying size, opening off a central passage. There was a little washroom and a privy at the west corner of the flat, and a narrow room next to it may have been heated by hypocaust (i.e. by heat drawn from an external fireplace, through under-floor channels, so warming the floor). It is likely that the century's office and record-room would be located in the flat.

The contrast between the centurion's quarters and the men's accommodation may not strike visitors until they realise that the pairs of rooms, front and back, that make up the rest of the block each housed as many as eight men. The vast difference between the ordinary second-century legionary on his 300 *denarii* a year and his centurion on 5,000 is nowhere more cogently illustrated than by these arrangements. In the field-camp, a ten-foot square tent housed that number of men, forming a *contubernium* or mess; but as some may have been reckoned as being on duty, eight sleeping places need not necessarily have been provided. In the permanent block, of course they were; and the inner room or dormitory, almost 4 m square, could certainly accommodate them on the floor. Some barracks, not these, have fireplaces for winter heating; and it may be that braziers of charcoal were allowed here. In that case double-decker bunks may have been installed to make more floor-space available; but there is no evidence on the point. The outer room of each pair was used as a living-room and for personal equipment. Heavy equipment belonging to the century probably went into one of the rampart storehouses near by.

According to the ancient source *De Munitionibus Castrorum*, ten eight-man tents housed a century, which was thus of 80 men. At Caerleon, however, there are twelve *contubernia* (perhaps thirteen in XVII), and figures in other fortresses exceed the minimal ten. The additional two pairs probably housed the century's due proportion of non-combattant headquarters staff and possibly two of the legion's 120 mounted scouts (*equites*), for none of whom there seems to have been separate accommodation. If we add in a few soldiers' servants or slaves (*calones, lixae*) we can readily reach the figure of some 600 men for each ordinary cohort, the 'computed figure' according to the author of the above-mentioned work, that is 120 more than the nominal 480 reached by multiplying the figure of 80 by six (being the number of centuries in a cohort). However, it is doubtful whether each century was normally at full strength, and conditions in barracks would probably have been rather more agreeable than the computation suggests. It is also possible that the three under-officers of each century, the *optio* or administrative second-in-command, the *signifer* or standard-bearer, and the *tesserarius* or orderly, were lodged with the *centurio*.

The accommodation of the first cohort (XIV) is difficult to understand without further excavation. However, the large houses of three of the five centurions who commanded its six centuries after the reduction in its size — the chief centurion (*primus pilus*) commanded two — are clear enough. The plan shows that they were arranged around internal courtyards, and occupied about twice the floor-area of an ordinary centurion's quarters, in recognition of the superior status of their occupants. We note, too, that they were walled off from the men's quarters and were separated from the *via principalis* by store-blocks.

The stone foundations in XXIII, Barrack 1, were not carried for more than a few courses above the ground, for the superstructure continued to be timber-framed; and the same is true of all other living-accommodation

Antefixes (gable-ornaments), heights 18 and 15 cm.

except for the legate's residence. The framework would have been filled in with panels of wattle-and-daub, rendered in stucco and whitewashed or coloured pink as a waterproofing measure. Sometimes we have evidence of a plastered interior painted in simple coloured designs as well.

The roof-structure was certainly massive, for the tiles (*tegulae*) were large and heavy, well over 10 kg apiece, not to mention the half-cylindrical tiles (*imbrices*) covering the joints between the rows; the pitch was low. There were ornamental gable-tiles (*antefixa*) bearing emblems to which a protective significance attached, dolphins, or mainly gorgon's heads, thought to attract evil and so to deflect it from the occupants; they have various celestial symbols in the corners — wheels, stars, crosses etc. Only one antefix carries the legion's title, and none the legion's emblems, the capricorn or the Pegasus. Legions are fairly evenly divided as to whether their emblems appear on antefixes; thus the Twentieth's boar is the commonest motif on antefixes made at Holt. The barrack-windows were sometimes glazed in thick panes of blue-green (natural) hue, probably cast on the spot from broken bottles and vessels. The floors were variously of clay, gravel, concrete or boards.

Officers' Houses (X, etc.)

Enough is known of the house on the Museum site to show that, as elsewhere, it was from the first of courtyard plan like the houses of the centurions of the first cohort, but larger; the house on the Museum site boasted small private baths, and all may have done so, the plans in general being no doubt very similar.

Legate's Residence (XX)

This building is very imperfectly known, but it was in massive masonry, the design centring upon a paved area containing a round-ended pool — not a mere sunken garden, as has been claimed as the explanation of the similar (but badly preserved) features in both *praetoria* at the double-legion fortress of Xanten on the Rhine. Another somewhat smaller pool figures on the plan of the 'Castle' baths at Caerleon, but it does not seem very likely that the pool now in question was for swimming. An ornamental pool, with an additional apse in the middle of one side, occupied the court of the governor's palace at London, with the fragmentary plan of which our own walling seems otherwise to have much in common.

Administrative and Other Buildings — Headquarters (XV)

Most of the *principia* lies beneath the churchyard, where finds include the Severian inscription (p.34) and a mosaic of labyrinth design, of which the surviving portion is reset in the Museum. A statuette of a presiding spirit (*Genius*) of some grade of headquarters staff, whose meeting-place (*schola*) the mosaic-floored room was, came to light at the same time.

Behind the great *forum*-courtyard lined with offices, *scholae* and armouries lay the great hall (*basilica*), almost 64.5 m long and 25 m wide, with massive foundations and column-bases; however, it may never have

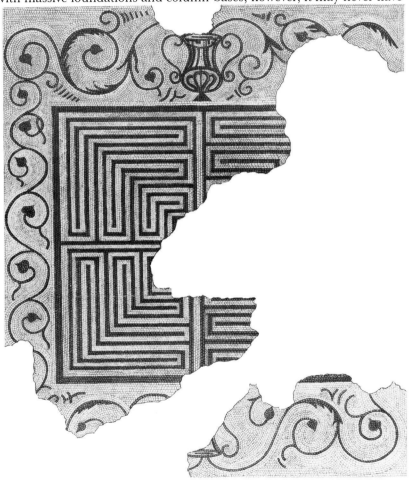

Labyrinth mosaic from a room in the N.E. forum *range of the Headquarters. Churchyard, 1865.*

Statuette of a Genius *or presiding spirit, holding a palm-decked* cornucopiae *symbolizing prosperous victories. Height 40 cm. Headquarters (Churchyard, 1865).*

been built-up, for a thin, hard-trodden soil overlay the nave, aisles, and colonnade-foundations alike, and no fragment of a capital from any of the columns was discovered. At either end of this space was a raised *tribunal* or platform where officers heard criminal and other cases; that on the north-east was excavated. On the short axis of the building stood a railed enclosure about 3.5 m square, which had had double gates on the south-east. This feature is matched only at York, where it is late, as it is here. It may have protected a main altar.

Along the rear or north-west side of the *basilica* lay the massive foundations of a row of chambers, four and four on either side of the central chapel of the standards (*aedes*), which was 11 m deep and almost 10 m wide with a raised floor and benches for statues along either side. Repairs effected *c.*176-80 may have extended to the erection of the columniated screen in front, where, with others, the pilasters inscribed in honour of the Birthday of the Eagle in 234 and 244 (p.37) will have stood. The chambers to either side of the *aedes* were probably treasuries (*aeraria*). Several statue-bases were identified, symmetrically placed in front of the screen; and one can imagine the main altar in its railed enclosure with this screen and these statues as a backdrop, through which are discerned the entrance to the chapel and the Eagle in pride of place at the rear.

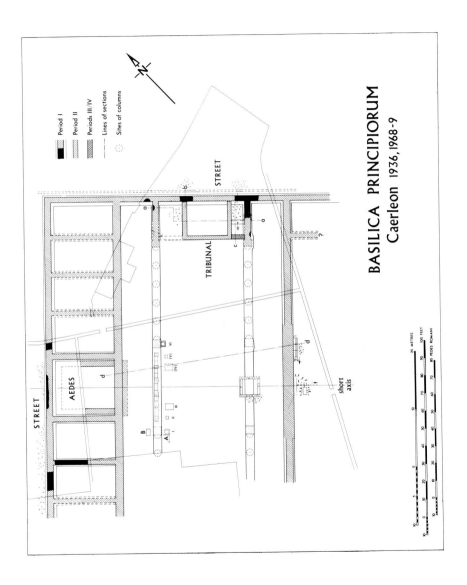

BASILICA PRINCIPIORUM
Caerleon 1936, 1968-9

The Hospital (VI)

This building (*valetudinarium*) has been slightly explored, and would have measured some 70 m square. It took the form of a double range of paired ward-cubicles — one room for every century — separated by a wide corridor, arranged around three sides of a large courtyard. A reception-hall or treatment-area was later constructed over part of the courtyard with access from the south-east.

The hospital was under the care of an *optio* on the camp-prefect's staff, controlling a number of orderlies or dressers. Enlisted medical personnel, even experienced surgeons, were classed merely as privileged rankers. The finest doctors might even be of servile status, Graeco-Asiatics like the two who have left inscriptions at Chester; but these were private employees of the commandant. Evidence from other fortresses suggests that the sick received special rations of wine and perhaps oil, and that medicinal herbs were grown in the courtyard. The Rhodian amphora (p.31), addressed to the Legion, may be understood in this sense: heavily salted, it had a laxative effect.

Workshops (XXI)

In Area XXI Caerleon possesses a good excavated example of a legionary *fabrica*. The plan is of the courtyard type, with large halls for manufacture or storage on two sides, subdivided space on the third — including two blocks which much resemble centurion's flats and were probably living-accommodation for non-combattant craftsmen, particularly of the building trades, and the *optio fabricae* in charge of them. The fourth (north-east) side is not well known. Into the courtyard project further buildings, of which two are L-shaped residential units for workmen, possibly includ.ng civilians or slaves. The steeping-tank for leather-preparation, of which the lead strapwork survived and is shown in a photograph, was excavated in the remaining part of the courtyard, where further excavations produced evidence of lead-working on a large scale, probably in connexion with the water-distribution system of the fortress. Area XVI and Area XIX also held *fabricae*, in all probability; much iron-smithing went on adjacent to the large *basilica* in XIX. (XVI has also been identified as a stable; but, as the original excavators of 1908 pointed out, a step of nearly half a metre into a stable is hardly conducive to that opinion.) As regards other manufacturing facilities at Caerleon, it is clear that part of the long rampart-building on the north-west side, of third-century date, was used to manufacture composite bows, scabbards, and other items appropriate to an auxiliary garrison, rather than a legionary one.

Lead strapwork covering the joints between the boards of a steeping-tank 1.6 by 3.2 m,
Fabrica *(Jenkins' Field, 1928).*

The Fortress Baths (V)

The *thermae* are treated only in outline here. Part of the cold hall
(*frigidarium*) and the swimming-bath (*natatio*) are preserved under cover
for public inspection at the rear of the car-park near the Bull Inn.

The core of cold, warm and hot halls (*frigidarium, tepidarium* and
caldarium) is arranged in a simple linear sequence or row, measuring
some 47 by 21.5 m overall. This block follows an architecturally-advanced
design far removed from the structures hitherto discussed. Each of the
halls had a span of 40 Roman feet (11.8 m) and a length of 19.6 m, a
figure which results from the circular geometry within which the plan was
described; the logical concomitant was a vaulted superstructure like the
frigidarium of the baths at Paris, still existing as part of the Musée Cluny.
As the diagram shows, the north-west and south-east ends of the main
block served to buttress the vaults, their own massivity however being
reduced by the apsidal and rectangular recesses which they contain. In
the *frigidarium* these recesses were all pools in the later history of the
building, but the original design placed freestanding splash-basins (*labra*)
in the apses. A Purbeck Marble *labrum* in the form of a great round shield
with a gorgon's head at the centre, found in the 'Castle' baths, is
exhibited in the Fortress Baths cover-building to give an idea of what the

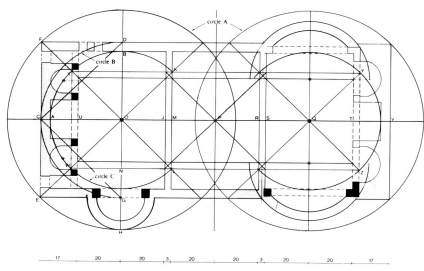

Diagram to show the circular geometry of the main block of the Fortress Baths.

labra would have been like. The same site supplies a monolithic pierced sink-cover, shown near the drain at the centre of the *frigidarium* which now lacks its own; it is to the right or south-east side of the cover-building (which therefore extends over only half of the Roman hall, a good indication of its huge size). Here bathers would have stood for a shower to freshen up after their spell in the *caldarium*; attendants or friends would have poured water over them. We can imagine the great height of the *frigidarium* and the two other halls, 14.5 m from floor to vaulted ceiling painted in *trompe l'oeil* coffers.

This building has its place in the gradual development of the concrete vaulted architecture which was to reach its zenith in the second-century buildings of Rome itself. Among earlier parallels, baths at *Vindonissa* in Switzerland and what is known of the Second Augustan's baths at its former base at Exeter are important, and baths at the Roman colony of *Aventicum* (Avenches), about contemporary, are among those exhibiting a striking affinity of plan. However, the plan-geometry at Caerleon is more advanced.

Before many years had passed, the swimming-bath (*natatio*) was installed in the colonnaded exercise-yard (*palaestra*) on the south-west of the main block. It was 41 m long, nearly 6.5 m wide and 1.2 to 1.6 m deep, with a fountain-house (*nymphaeum*) at the north-west end, containing the steps for a cascade: we may remember that in Roman times the water-supply was continuous, like the natural springs and streams tapped. The battered remains of a Bath Stone dolphin, perhaps mounted here as part of a sculpture-group, delivered water through its mouth. Later, the *natatio* was shortened to a mere 25.5 m, the blocking-walls both being visible in the cover-building. The leaden outlet-pipe will be noticed at the south-east end.

About the same time — in the early 80's — a covered exercise-hall (*basilica*) 64.5 m long and 24 m wide was laid out between the main block of the baths and the *via principalis*, projecting therefore across the row of officers' houses, which may have been left incomplete. Indeed there is reason to suspect that this large hall, with its 12 m nave separated from the 6 m aisles by 17 brick-built columns on either side, may (like the *basilica principiorum*) never have been completed: it had no proper floor, and part of its south-west wall was knocked down to make room for the double furnace of a heated apartment on that side of the bath-building. Another addition to the main block was a heated room floored with mosaic, about 9.5 m square, perhaps a dressing-room (*apodyterium*), though fitted with a hypocaust. A piece of the mosaic, found as long ago as 1877 when drains were laid in Backhall-st., has been preserved and is

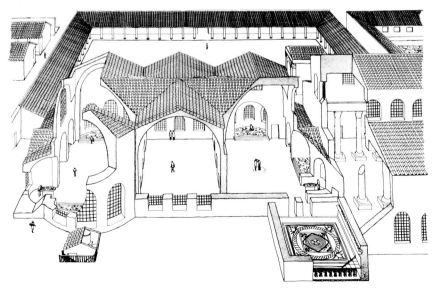

Cut-away view of the Fortress Baths, from the N.E.

now mounted on the far wall of the cover-building close to its original site. The subject was diagonally-crossed spears disguised with greenery and streamers as Bacchic wands (*thyrsi*), overlaid by concentric circles making up a great round shield. The use of spears rather than wands for the *thyrsi* refers to the story of Bacchus, who so armed his attendants in order to outwit enemies who would fall on his joyous procession.

Among the many finds throwing light on the life of the baths are two strigils, one very plain, and one inlaid with the labours of Hercules in gold, brass and silver — one of a set, and very rare; these instruments were used to scrape clean the skin. Also found were fragments of glass bottles which had contained the oil used for massage; little glass or pottery cups; and pig, sheep and chicken-bones from the snacks consumed. A separate guidebook describes the many engraved gems from finger-rings, found in the silt of the frigidarium drain, where they had collected having fallen from their settings. These 88 stones are the largest accumulation recovered from any Romano-British site so far explored, and recall a similar but smaller assemblage from the baths of Bath. Finds of jewellery and even of milk-teeth show that the baths were at times open to womenfolk and children, and a small leaden admission-ticket was also discovered, probably for civilian use.

Camp-building on Trajan's Column: turf-faced earthen ramparts, timber superstructures and gateways: notice the wide embrasures, the openwork towers (top left), where leather tents can be seen within. The scene demonstrates also the flexibility of the legionary armour, manifestly suitable for working in.

The Defences and Adjuncts

The defences can never have been attacked in the mainly peaceful region which South Wales became soon after the completion of the conquest in the middle 70's, though trouble across the Bristol Channel is indicated by a Bath inscription which shows that a regional centurion had had to be appointed, presumably from our legion, in the second or third century. Almost from the start, the rampart and then the wall were overshadowed by the adjacent Amphitheatre, which in hostile hands would have commanded a wide area within the enclosure. The wall is best preserved opposite the Amphitheatre and down to the south corner, where it stands over 3.5 m high, within a metre of the original height of the parapet-walk, if indications at Chester and York may be applied here. The character of the masonry and its mortar change towards the south corner, because there the wall was rebuilt owing to weak ground. Within, the foundations of two turrets, one in the corner, appear: they are 4.0 by 4.5 m externally, and would have been carried up one storey above the parapet-walk, thus to 7 or 8 m, in order to provide a raised fighting-platform or sentry-box. The ground-floor chambers were soon used as rubbish-holes, and were blocked-off, so that cook-houses (replacing the open-air ovens of which remains can be seen along the *intervallum* in Area XXIII, paired like the centurial barracks) could be built against them. Furthermore, excavations on the north-west rampart in XXIII showed that at least two interval-turrets had been knocked down when rampart storehouses were erected *c.*120; the remainder there seem to have been destroyed when a large magazine was erected towards the year 200.

Little is known of the gates, designed with double passageways* flanked by towers presumably of the same height as the interval and corner-turrets — there was no reason to make them higher. The one tower explored was, as explained above, a rebuild of 215(?), and no original plan is known. The north-east gate seems to have been narrowed about the same time, and the wall adjacent rebuilt behind the original line — but the findings are incomplete and very obscure in consequence.

Just past the south corner, the remains of an arched sewer to carry the effluent from a latrine inside will be perceived. There were probably latrines in all four corners, and that in the west corner is exposed. Notice the rounded corners of the drain, over which a 12 m run of wooden seating would have been arranged. The wall apparently dividing the building into two has, however, nothing to do with it: it is of earlier date, belonging to a rampart storehouse superseded when the latrine was built

* A few of the great Bath Stone voussoirs from the south-west gate, indicating passages 3.6 m wide, are to be seen near the site of their discovery, beside the wall.

about the middle of the second century. Traces of the latrine pavement, with edging gutter, still survive; on this pavement would have stood the tub containing the sponges used instead of toilet-paper. The equivalent stone basin remains in the latrine at Housesteads fort on Hadrian's wall; as for sponges, they are in archaeological evidence at York, spicules being found in the filling of the sewer leading from the fortress-baths there. At Caerleon the small angular chamber next to the latrine seems to have contained a tank for flushing purposes; the outfall-drain led at no great depth beside the adjacent barrack, hardly a very sanitary arrangement.

Latrine, W. corner, 1929, as restored.

The Amphitheatre

The *ludus* was laid out on a short axis of 140 Roman feet (41.3 m). Reference was made to the manner in which the building, some 83 by 63 m, was squeezed into the space between an existing bath-house (which was modified in consequence) and the fortress-ditch (which was half-filled where the structure came closest to it). The new rounded corner of the baths and the new furnace-arch can be seen, but nothing now of the later food-hall (*macellum*) built on the site of the baths.

The amphitheatre was constructed on ground shelving to the south, the excavation of the arena being taken to a level bottom where, fortunately, the subsoil was sandy and provided a suitable surface: later it was given a stony metalling. The spoil was mostly dumped in the south quadrant to build up the seating-bank there. A drain on the long axis still carries off ground-water to the Usk, and the gutter round the bottom of the arena-wall ran into it. The arena-wall was accurately laid out and stood about 3.7 m high, capped with great half-cylindrical stones such as

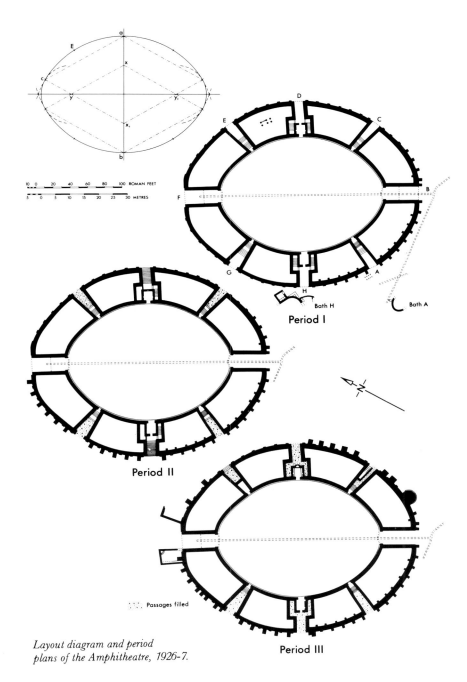

E

10 0   20   40   60   80   100 ROMAN FEET
5   0   5   10   15   20   25   30 METRES

Period I

Bath H

Bath A

Period II

Passages filled

Period III

*Layout diagram and period
plans of the Amphitheatre, 1926-7.*

61

are stacked outside the south entrance (B). The outer wall was not so carefully laid out, giving a width of 12.3 to 13.6 m to the banks; but the visitor will notice the buttresses around it, especially in the south quadrant* but carried round the whole periphery as pilasters; these give us a clue as to the superstructure. On the south, if he is tall enough, he will also notice the alternately-spaced buttresses, on the inside of the outer wall, missing elsewhere but here deemed necessary because, as stated above, the spoil from the arena was embanked on this side. Several wall-stones inscribed with the names of the centuries responsible for the work were discovered; they were destined to be covered by the mortar rendering. One exception is the handsome tablet of Lias limestone found re-used — as most of the others had been — in later work which has preserved the original red-lead paint of the lettering: 'Century of Rufinius'. From another of the 'centurial stones' we learn that the century of Rufinius Primus belonged to the third cohort.

South quadrant of the Amphitheatre, showing buttresses and vertical kerb-stone. Excavated 1926-7.

There are eight entrances. The two *portae pompae* or processional entrances giving access to the arena, B and F (the visitor enters by F) are unusual in having been designed with their sides parallel with the long axis rather than radial to the elliptical arena. As at other entrances, the visitor will notice the massive stones of the gate-piers both at the outer

*Stumps remain of the large stones set edgewise to protect the buttresses from wheeled traffic near Entrance A.

periphery and about halfway down the passageway: the inclined barrel-vaults which at first existed in all the entrances stopped short at this medial point (the line of the rake of the vault is very clear in Entrance B, and if one continues it down to the intersection of the arena-wall, it will be realised that the opening would have been absurdly low). The springers of the outer arches remain in both these entrances, showing that the outer wall rose over 4 m above the outside ground-level, 7.5 m above the level of the arena to the underside of the arches; this was by no means the full height of the structure.

The two entrances on the short axis (D and H) include at arena-level a square chamber with access from the rear — i.e. from the bottom of the flight of steps leading down from the exterior. Branching steep steps to either side led in one case to the box erected above the basement chambers (where gladiators and other performers probably waited their turn) and in the other case to the front of the seating. The four minor entrances are very complicated as now exposed, but originally all had the same plan of (1) a deep flight of steps down, and from it (2) a steep flight, under which beast-dens were contrived, up to the front of the seating. The outer stone thresholds, with the holes to take the pivots of the gates, remain exposed.

Stone commemorating work by the Century of Rufinius. From the Amphitheatre, 1956.

Later in the history of the building, the barrel-vaults were removed, and the entrances, except for the *portae pompae*, were filled level with the ground outside in consequence, it appears, of flooding. Much of the calcareous tufa — a very porous white stone* — used in the vaults was re-employed in later work, notably in the two entrances on the short axis. Semicircular steps near Entrance B are part of the latest arrangements for access to the seating.

Turning now to the superstructure, it is to be observed that the banks were never higher than today: their metalled surfaces have been found not far below the turf. Not a vestige of a stone seat occurred, and the arrangements were therefore of timber. Thus, on the bank between Entrances D and E, pits a metre square and deep for posts of 30 cm scantling have been detected. They held vertical members of an openwork grandstand as suggested in the reconstruction-drawing. Doubtless this was intended as a temporary measure, as perhaps in the case of an amphitheatre depicted on Trajan's Column at *Drobetae*, the Roman base on the Dacian side of the Danube bridge: the realisation that the lowest storey of this structure contained arched entrances and was therefore of stone has helped in the elucidation of the Caerleon building. In our case, the outermost ring of vertical members supporting the seating must have been bedded into sockets in the thickness (1.4—1.8 m) of the outer wall. The natural strains upon this type of construction, augmented by the vibrations caused by an excited audience, would in time have loosened the posts and thus weakened the wall, thick though it was; and this is the reason for the addition of more buttresses, for the most part in between the original buttresses or pilasters and generally of massive dimensions, especially on the east.

The function of this amphitheatre was various. In the first place, it would amply seat the entire legion on the rare occasions when the Emperor or the provincial Governor visited *Isca* — Hadrian, Geta and Carausius might have harangued the troops from one of the boxes on the short axis. The arena also served for weapon-training where stakes could be set up against which recruits practised combat, armed with wooden swords and wickerwork shields. But chiefly the arena witnessed the degenerate and bloody pastimes of all such monuments, preceded though they were by the rites and ceremonies proper to the days on which they were held. A small leaden ticket from this amphitheatre, stamped with the number XIII, since it can hardly refer either to a bank

---

* Formed by the deposition of hard-water springs in limestone country, often around leaves, sticks, etc., the impression of which it preserves. Very light because of its vesicular nature, calcareous tufa reminded the Romans of the volcanic sort.

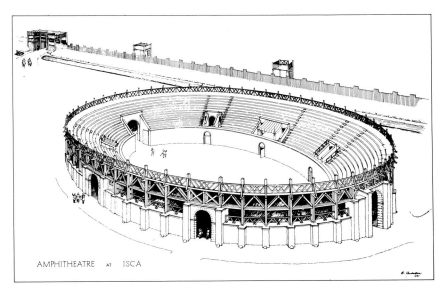

The Amphitheatre. Drawn by Robert Anderson, 1981.

Amphitheatre with wooden staging above the ground storey, at Drobetae. *Trajan's Column.*

of seats or a single seat, may reflect evidence from elsewhere to indicate the inordinate length of time to which games might be protracted under the Empire — thirteen days or more.

A stone from one of the buttresses on the south side relates to gladiatorial combat. In the centre a trident is shown, as used by net-fighters (*retiarii*); on either side a curious gabled shape represents the shoulder-piece (*galerus*) worn by them, on which to hitch the net and the cord to which it was attached. Palm-fronds of victory close the design.

Stone from the Amphitheatre, showing the trident and shoulder-pieces of a Net-fighter, between victory palms. Width, 40 cm.

Another find to be mentioned is a small square piece of lead bearing a dedication to the Goddess of Fate, Nemesis, regularly invoked at amphitheatres; at Chester a small shrine containing an altar dedicated to her stood near one of the main entrances, opening off the arena. Possibly the chamber in our Entrance D was turned into a Nemeseum in the third century, when the attractive brick niche visible in its back wall was formed; more probably, the shrine of this goddess, as at *Carnuntum*, lay to one side of the approach to Entrance F. The inscription is a curse, devoting to Nemesis a stolen cloak and boots — perhaps from the dressing-room in the baths near by.

Whether there were resident, or merely visiting, companies of gladiators and other entertainers such as acrobats must remain obscure. Not the least strange item in a list of soldiers with special skills, who were excused fatigue-duties, is *gladiatores*. The entry in Justinian's *Digest* of Roman law dates back to a jurist of the second century, and so may well have applied at Caerleon; one is reminded that gladiators had their fans (*amatores*) as a sad epitaph from Verona indicates, commemorating a man who fell in his eighth fight at the age of 23: '. . . I advise you not to put your faith in Nemesis — I was deceived that way.' The hinterland of Caerleon would also have provided all sorts of game including bears, wolves and wildcats among others, as indeed the restoration of Diana's temple by a grateful hunter might suggest. A possible wolf's bone is among the finds from the amphitheatre.

The Caerleon Martyrs

The Catholic church near the bridge at Caerleon is dedicated to SS. David — patron saint of Wales — Julius and Aaron. The latter two are with Alban and an early bishop of London, 'Augulus', the first martyrs of the Christian faith in Britain. No account of the amphitheatre is complete without reference to Julius and Aaron, though in truth we know no more than their names, being the only details surviving in popular tradition at the time of Gildas, who wrote in the sixth century, and is copied in this particular by Bede. Gildas names the two as 'citizens of the city of the Legions': that Caerleon rather than Chester or even York is meant is proved by a charter collected into the *Book of Llandaff* and assignable to *c*.864, wherein mention is made of their *martyrium*, or shrine in their honour. Indeed, the place name of St. Julian's, on the left bank of the Usk towards Newport, depends on this local link.

The date and condition of the two are elusive and must remain uncertain. Opinion tends to favour the savage persecution of the middle of the third century rather than the later persecution under Diocletian, from which Britain seems to have escaped. By or during the third century, Christianity had spread deeply through the army, and there are various martyrdoms on record in which soldiers — even a recruit or a veteran — fail to abide by the military oath, disgrace their uniform, or refuse, on Christian grounds, to accept the brand or tattoo which (in late times) signified admittance to the ranks. There must be a grain of truth in these stories, which take the form rather of homilies. Perhaps Julius was a legionary: the name is suggestive, a very common one. Aaron sounds Jewish; he may have been a trader in the *canabae* and a member of a small Christian fellowship centred on the fortress or perhaps Bulmore, high above which is the reputed site of the *martyrium*. No further evidence of Christianity is known from Caerleon, and at Caerwent the evidence is no earlier than the late fourth century: however, the purely archaeological record of Roman Britain yields nothing certainly Christian of a date earlier than the Peace of the Church in 313.

It was normal for those condemned to death to meet their end by the sword, if citizens, in the amphitheatres of the Roman world; but if Julius and Aaron were executed in the Caerleon arena, it cannot have been by the authority of the legionary legate, who had no power of the death-penalty, which rested with the provincial governor as the deputy of the emperor. There is no reason to think that the chamber in Entrance D was ever a *martyrium*.

Silver tip from a vexillum *or banner. 33 cm. School Field, 1928.*

Bibliography

Most of the references to the fortress and its suburbs earlier than 1972 will be found in the present writer's *Isca* (National Museum of Wales, 1972); the Amphitheatre is published in *Archaeologia*, vol. lxxviii, 1928. Later references will be found in *Britannia*, a journal of the Society for the Promotion of Roman Studies; in the Cambrian Archaeological Association's *Archaeologia Cambrensis* and in vol. i of its *Monographs & Collections*, 1978; the *Bulletin* of the Board of Celtic Studies of the University of Wales; and the *Annual Reports* of the Glamorgan-Gwent Archaeological Trust. The most recent study of a building is J.D. Zienkiewicz, *The Legionary Fortress Baths at Caerleon*, 2 vols. (National Museum of Wales and Cadw: Welsh Historic Monuments, 1986). Land-reclamation, partly in *Britannia*, 1986.

The standard collection of inscriptions from the site down to 1954 is in R.G. Collingwood and R.P. Wright, *The Roman Inscriptions of Britain*, vol. i (1965); additions will be found in the *Journal of Roman Studies* down to 1969, and in *Britannia* from 1970 onwards. Sculptured stones are described by R.J. Brewer in *Corpus Signorum Imperii Romani, Great Britain*, vol. i fasc. 5, *Wales* (British Academy, 1986). The *antefixa* and brick and tile-stamps are described by G.C. Boon in *Laterarium Iscanum* (National Museum of Wales, 1984). Bread-stamps, dies and tags are included in V.E. and A.H. Nash-Williams, *Cat. Roman Inscribed and Sculptured Stones found at Caerleon, Mon.* (National Museum of Wales, 1935).

There is no up-to-date compendious account of military aspects of Roman Wales. Much work has gone on since 1969, when the second edition of Nash-Williams's *The Roman Frontier in Wales* (first published 1954) was produced under the editorship of M.G. Jarrett for the Eighth International Congress of Roman Frontier Studies held partly in Wales that year. The early ('Usk') period is well-covered by W.H. Manning in Part I of *Report on the Excavations at Usk 1965-1976, The Fortress Excavations 1968-1971* (Board of Celtic Studies, 1981). Among articles in the journals cited above and others, note J.L. Davies' brief reappraisal of 'Roman military deployment in Wales . . . from Claudius to the Antonines' in *Roman Frontier Studies 1979*, Papers presented to the 12th International Congress of Roman Frontier Studies, ed. W.S. Hanson and L.J.F. Keppie (BAR Internat. Ser. 71, 1980).

For Roman Britain the forthcoming new edition of S.S. Frere's *Britannia* (first published 1967) is important. There is much detail, sensibly discussed, in P. Salway's *Roman Britain* (Oxford History of England,

1981). An excellent small book is Malcolm Todd's *Roman Britain 55 B.C.-A.D. 400* (Fontana Press, 1985); J.S. Wacher, *Roman Britain* (Dent, 1978, repr. 1986); for background take in e.g. Colin Wells, *The Roman Empire* (Fontana, 1984). A new edition of the Ordnance Survey *Map of Roman Britain* is expected (4th ed., 1978).

For the army, there is Graham Webster's *The Roman Imperial Army* (third ed., A. and C. Black, 1985); P.A. Holder, *The Roman Army in Britain* (Batsford, 1982); L. Keppie, *The Making of the Roman Army* (Batsford, 1984), and G.R. Watson, *The Roman Soldier* (Thames and Hudson, 1969, repr. 1983). For practical details see Peter Connolly's well-illustrated *The Roman Army* (Macdonald Educational, 1975). Note also Anthony Birley, *The People of Roman Britain* (Batsford, 1979), and his *Fasti of Roman Britain* (Clarendon Press, 1981). M. Junkelmann, *Die Legionen des Augustus* (Philipp von Zabern, 1986), wider than its subject, is also recommended, as is L. Wierschowski, *Heer und Wirtschaft* (Bonn, 1984). Medical service, R.W. Davies, *Saalburg-Jahrbuch*, xxvii, 1970; but J.F. Gilliam, *Roman Army Papers* (1986), 1ff. for the status of enlisted doctors.

For fortresses and forts see Anne Johnson, *Roman Forts* (A. and C. Black, 1983); D.J. Breeze, *Roman Forts in Britain* (Shire Publns., 1983); and works cited above. The only authoritative general discussion of the buildings of a legionary fortress is H. von Petrikovits, *Die Innenbauten römischer Legionslager während der Prinzipatszeit* (Abhandlungen der rheinisch-westfälischen Akademie der Wissenschaften, Band 56, 1975). Sections in L.F. Pitts and J.K. St.Joseph, *The Roman Fortress at Inchtuthil* (Britannia Monographs, No. 6, 1986) are important, notably the discussion of the first cohort's accommodation. See also P. Carrington, 'The Plan of the Legionary Fortress at Chester, a Reconsideration' in *Chester Archaeological Journal*, vol. 68, 1986, and the detailed archaeology of Chester by D. Petch in *The Victoria History of the County of Chester*, vol. i (Inst. of Historical Research, 1987). Papers by F. Vittinghof deal with aspects of legionary land-holdings, *canabae*, etc., in *I diritti locali nelle provincie romane* (Academia Nazionale dei Lincei, Anno ccclxxi, 1974, Quaderno N.194); *Chiron* i (1971); and *Legio vii Gemina* (Leon, 1970). Note also H. von Petrikovits in *Actes du vii* Congrès international d'Épigraphie grecque et latine 1977* (Constanza, 1979).

G.R. Stephens, 'Caerleon and the Martyrdom of SS. Aaron and Julius', in *Bulletin* of the Board of Celtic Studies, vol. xxxii (1985) is the most recent treatment of this subject; on Alban's connexion, see W. Levison, *Antiquity*, vol.xv (1941).

Fragment, 42 cm wide, of a 10th-century cross-slab found in Caerleon churchyard about 1854, drawn by J.E. Lee, founder of the Roman Legionary Museum. The original is in the National Museum of Wales, Cardiff. Above the bird-like angels appears part of the curved 'wheel' of the cross-head, with the bottom arm of the cross showing to the right, above a panel of similar interlaced work. Other slabs of this kind are known from Bulmore (N.M.W.) and St. Arvans near Chepstow (more complete; in church).